To my dad who always believed in me,

even when I lost hope.

Contents

Part 1

Knowing love

PART 2

Revival

PART 1

Knowing

Love

1

A lot like love

When you start getting attracted to someone, you feel that this is what is love. You start thinking that this relationship is going to last a lifetime. Some of you might have even just wanted it to last for some time at least.

You think it is love because it is a lot like love.

It is a lot like what you have read in those love stories. It is a lot like what you have watched in the movies.

What no one tells you is that love in real life is nothing like that. Not even close.

While growing up, all that we have read in fairytales is sheer lies.

Stop thinking it is love because the prince has finally arrived and rescued you. You are not anyone's object of pity.

Stop feeling that you are privileged because he has chosen you.

You are divine.

You are a blessing.

You are the child of the universe.

The core of love is you don't think you are in love, you feel it.

You don't have to think if you have made the right move by letting him into your life.

You will not be assuming that it is love because you both fight a lot.

I often hear people say fights are common for any relationship. It is okay to compromise on yourself respect for the one you love.

No, IT IS NOT.

In love, fights are not common on a regular basis. Abuse is not common. Self-respect is valuable.

Do not tell yourself it is love if you are crying yourself to sleep every day.

Do not tell yourself it is love if it is you who is the only one working on this relationship.

Do not tell yourself it is love if you have to always put up with giving space to him as he is scared of letting you in even after you have shown him love.

Do not call it love if it is you who is left broken more and more within after each argument.

Do not call it love if it makes you feel miserable in even being alive.

What you have in your life can be a lot like love. But it is definitely not love.

Because real love demands work.

It demands care.

It needs trust.

It needs effort.

It needs compromise. But from both the sides.
Any relationship consists of two people so any effort from
one person will be futile.

You cannot save this relationship.
You can only save yourself from the trauma you go through
every day.

What you are feeling at the moment is a lot like love, but it is not
love.

Because when love finds you it won't be a maybe or perhaps;
it is going to be a place far away from the temporary abode.

And I fell hopelessly for an angel

Not once did I think I would lose my wings

To give peace to my lover

Who only blessed me with storms

Under the illusion of something called love

A lot like love yet nothing like it

2

Perfection

Often I see people wonder what is a perfect relationship like. Everyone strives to make their relationships perfectly happy, perfectly blissful and perfectly harmonious.

Many times we fail to understand why our relationships with our parents can't be perfect, why can't we have that perfect lover. What we mortals don't understand that nothing is perfect in life.

Not your parents, not your siblings, not your boyfriend, not your husband and darling, not even you. But love can be perfect and relationships can be perfect too if you can accept that it is already perfect.

It is you who can see perfection in the imperfect also.

It doesn't have to be a "flawless" lover that hurts you in the end.

Rather it can be a person who is flawed but chooses to love you irrespective of your setbacks.

It is all about your perspective.

If you believe in everything being perfect, it is already perfect.

It depends upon you on what you choose to have in your life.

You can keep chasing them and trying to make yourself into "their type". But would that make you feel content?

You can also try achieving "the perfect partner" standards or there is another option.

You can be who you are without having to change or be perfect in his eyes.

In the eyes of the right man, you will already be perfect despite your imperfections.

Sometimes we have perfection right in front of us, yet we don't see it.

We are too consumed by the general theory of how love should be and cannot accept how it really should be.

The universe decides to set us up with wrong partner who was perfect in our eyes and it keeps us stuck there till we do not realize the real meaning of what a perfect relationship is.

We are so hell bent on achieving the standards of perfection that we don't even receive the love we get with open arms just because it not from the one we want it to be.

Don't look for someone perfect, let the imperfect perfect love find you.

3

He Calls You Crazy

You give your 100 percent to this relationship. You fall in love with him to an extent where your life revolves around him. Sometimes you sacrifice having time for yourself too just to be there for him.

If he wants something, you are always there for him. You invest so much love and loyalty in this relationship that he is your sole priority.

Slowly he starts pushing you away.

He stops taking your calls, stops replying to your and calls you crazy for expecting too much out of him.

Trust me, he is right.

You are crazy for obviously chasing the wrong man, for however much you run after him he is only going to distance himself.

The more you try to prove you love him, the more he is going to hate you for even trying to communicate.

You start thinking maybe you are actually acting crazy and you should mellow down a bit and let him be for some time.

Your mind starts to work in the pattern where you start believing what he is telling you. If he says you should not expect him to be there for you all the time, you start agreeing.

Everything he asks of you, you always give in.

What you don't see is you are not a mere object to be used and thrown away at his convenience.

You are a lot more than that.

You are made of fire in your soul and courage in your veins.

You are meant to be crazy in love, not "crazy" as he terms you to be.

You are perfectly normal for wishing for love. For showing the love. For always being there for people. Because you do that especially when they don't deserve it .

The right partner will never find happiness in criticizing you or even calling you crazy because he knows what you are made up of.

He knows your essence and he will hold on to that without demanding any alteration.

4

Why Force?

Many a times I notice that people tend to force relationships.

Yes, you broke up.
Yes, it hurts.

Yes, you can cry. Yes, you should cry. Cry your heart out. Cry so much that you never cry again for the same reason.

In relationships, everything is not black and white. Love is not supposed to be right. It isn't supposed to be wrong.

There is only one tried and tested true fact. You are either happy or sad. There are no two opinions about it. If that relationship drains you or makes you overthink, you don't need this added stress in your life.

There are too many mediocre things in life anyway, the love you receive should not be one of them.

You cannot keep forcing him to love you. You cannot force him to be with you. If this takes you time to understand then take your time but make yourself understand this.

Understand it is not healthy to force anyone into choosing you.

You do not need such a love.
You do not want such a love.
This love will not uplift you. It will just laugh at your ruins over and over again.

You cannot force plants to grow in dead soil

You cannot expect flowers to bloom where there is no rain

You cannot force your heart to bear this pain of loss of

self-respect. You should not. You must not.

Someone that isn't yours from the beginning is bound to leave sooner or later.

You can only force one thing and that is to let it all be. Try detaching yourself from him.

Effort can't be asked for and if you have to force him to love you then that's not love, it is your weakness.

If you can drop yourself respect just to have them in your life, you will feel worse when they are back into your life.

You are not any consolation prize

You have so much to offer to the universe

You cannot depend on someone who fails to understand
you

You cannot let them have you and end you too

You are strong and you're beautifully carved

You need a partner to grow with, spiritually in love.
Not any one who has other intentions for you.
Not anyone who thinks loving you is too much
hard work.

Forcing them to love you is just portraying your
vulnerability to your partner.

5

Lying To Yourself

When he lies once, you tell yourself it is fine. It will not happen again. It is okay for people to lie sometimes. And then sometimes gradually turns into many times. When he says he is busy and he does not have time for you, you believe him.

When he says he cannot take your calls, you keep waiting for his call all day. But the phone never rings. This is the vibe that you need to identify with. You do not have to justify his excuses.

His schedule has time for everyone but you.

You start telling yourself that you should be more patient as that's what lovers do. He doesn't give you attention but you assume that's only because he is preoccupied with something maybe. He says he can't come over for dinner and you assume that you should give him space.

You do not have to feed your soul with all these lies and the betrayal because your soul needs soothing.

Your soul needs compassion. It only knows the language of love. Do not teach it to learn new languages of lies and deception.

You should know that it is not okay for him to cancel on you.

It is not okay for him to take you for granted.

It's never okay to be in love and yet feel such a void within you.

It is never okay to let him have a home in your soul when he couldn't even give you the shelter of his arms.

6

Maybe I Am Wrong

A lot of women come up to me and tell me how I can help them change their appearance. They ask me what they should be doing to look more enticing or more appealing or should they go for a makeover to attract him.

My answer to all of that is very simple. Yes, you should change. You should change your perception.

Change your vision.

Nothing is wrong with you how you look. But it's time to make a change in the way you think. You're beautiful the way you are.

If you want to lose weight, do it for yourself, you want to change your appearance only do it for yourself. If you want to change anything about yourself to impress someone, that person isn't worth your time.

It is time you realize you're pretty in not only the way you look but also in the way you love.

Your scars are beautiful

Your laughter is surreal

Your stretch marks are unique

If you have to be a different person in front of your lover, what is the point of being in a relationship.

If he cannot accept you just the way you are and is continuously complaining about how you look or what you eat and wants you to learn better ways to please him in bed while he cannot tolerate you pointing a finger at him, that is the most selfish man ever.

You are not born to be someone's slave in the bed or at home.

You deserve the respect he does not show you.

The right man will make you feel free with the touch of his fingers as well as caress your body with the warmth of his soul.

He will tell you every day that there is nothing wrong with you and moreover he will show his love along with words he speaks.

7

Cheating Is Okay

When he cheats on you for the first time and asks for forgiveness, you decide to forgive him out of love. You decide to look past this one incident and pretend you both are on the same page of love.

Then he again repeats it and this time, you think of ignoring it knowingly.

Darling, kindly pick up your bags and leave him. This is not important for him. It is more important for you.

Take all the courage you need in this world and be bold. A leopard never changes its spots.

Once he knows he has got the green card, he will do it again.

You are showing him the green card each time you are allowing him to come back into your life.

You are only acting like a safe back up option when you should be his priority.

You get emotional each time he says he loves you. There's a difference between saying sweet words and showing through action.

The right partner will never think of cheating as you are the only person he sees his home in.

You need to stop giving discounts to him because you are priceless and you possess a heart that's so rare.

You often wonder why he treats you the way he does. No longer you can feel the love that you once felt with him.

I let a man once cheat on me knowingly and in my heart I prayed so much it would stop.

The only thing that stopped were the subtle hints.

I used to wish so bad that the cheating would stop and I could stop forgiving him. But he knew one thing that I would stay no matter what.

The cheating never stopped. I had to make a choice. I stopped forgiving him. I made my move.

Sometimes the choices we make in life impact it in a major way.

You can choose to lead a life where everything seems good on the outside but it is made up of cracks from within.

But I stopped faking it.
I deserved that respect.
I deserved to smile.

But I chose to not be taken for granted.

I chose to forgive him one last time by forgiving myself to be with him.

8

Apology , Always

He makes mistakes and you keep apologizing on his behalf. He manipulates you into believing his sugar coated lies and you believe each and every word.

If you're with your friends, he makes you feel guilty of being without him. You start feeling apologetic for something that's not even your fault. So you learn to apologize for his mistakes as well as the times you aren't even wrong.

It's time you know that love is not supposed to manipulate you or make you feel sorry for living your life the way you want to.

No one can make you feel that way.

If you are always feeling sorry more than you are feeling the love with him then it's time for you to say goodbye for once and forever.

When my ex started playing mind games with me and manipulating me, he would often make me feel like it is my fault. I was not my usual self. Even if he forgot something, he would make me feel that it is due to me. Random fights that started over stupid topics turned into wars literally and we wouldn't talk to each other for weeks at a stretch.

We would only talk if I apologized. This relationship made me feel like I could never do anything right. That's when I realized that this is draining me mentally and this needs to stop for my good.

9

No More Fireworks

Any relationship that makes you feel so good in the beginning but as it progresses it you feel something is missing

. The blame games begin. He starts accusing you all the time. He doesn't Even if you're laughing he doesn't like the way you laugh.

You realize he does not know your favorite color anymore. His schedule is revolving more on meeting up with his friends and you slowly take a backseat in his schedule as well as his life.

All your plans are never appreciated and he has shifted from being "your confidante" to "your biggest critic"

He slowly starts disliking the same habits that he liked about you.

You start to feel neglected. You start feeling left out. You try communicating with him. It is all in vain. You feel that maybe you should spice things up and try to revive the spark.

But the true story is when its true then the spark doesn't just go away.

When you are in love, then it won't fade.

Just like the sky can be cast with clouds but doesn't lose its blue hue similarly real love will never leave you.

It isn't about the spark.

Love can never be boring as nothing can be more exciting than growing old together with the right person by your side.

You can try reading all those books on keeping it exciting in the bedroom, try bdsm or even have an amazing sex life but if sex was the answer then there wouldn't be so many divorces happening every day.

When you are with the right man, he will make love to your soul first and caress every corner of your mind, touch every inch of your heart.

You will feel so much peace in his arms that you will know that this is exactly where you belong.

10
Commitment Issues

When you are with someone, it is natural that there will come a point in your relationship when you will want to take things forward.

You bring up the topic of what the future holds or your ideas on marriage and he tries to change the topic or dissuade you from discussing any further. He keeps promising you to wait for him for another year.

This keeps going on for a long time. You start believing that maybe he will eventually marry you as he says. Honestly you are lying to yourself everyday by being with him. A good man won't take you and your love for granted. He will do all that it takes to put a label on the relationship because his focus is all about making you feel happier.

When men stray away from marriage or any commitment it is the beginning of another tale that's eventually going to end in a tragedy. He is not ready for any commitment at present and will neither be in the future because he does not value you yet. The right man will not fear having your precious heart and will cherish taking care of it.

My ex had major commitment issues. He was my best friend and that made it worse. I did not only lose a lover but also my best friend.

We were inseparable. When he saw me with others, his jealousy was obvious.

Many a times he tried telling me he loved me but all he could say was that he is not right for me. That angered me then. He had gone through a bad break up right before and I had helped him get over his ex.

Whenever I wanted any commitment from him, all I got was another excuse and the list was absurd. After a long time, I realized that I was just wasting my time.

You deserve much more than a guy who cannot give you any commitment.

It's never wrong to want a future with someone you love. And if he is busy making excuses to not put the ring on that finger, you can be busy making a life without him.

You are not responsible for his lack of commitment.

You cannot change a person's view on things so it is better to accept it exactly how it is and move on to a better life waiting ahead.

11

Fragile

If you pull a thread too much, it will eventually break. When all your effort is only one sided it will murder the love that you deserve to receive.

Love is innocent.

Relationships are fragile.

When you love someone you choose to show all your scars and your darkness without a second thought and when that only person decides to move away you feel helpless.

When something we don't expect happens then we can't usually come to terms with it.

More than our minds it's our souls that are so hurt deeply that somewhere you know you won't be whole again.

Deep down you knew he was not the right man for you but you chose to defy all odds just to be with him.

Trust is the most fragile thing that can build or end any relationship. Just like the sky would be so mundane without the stars, love is barren without the fundamentals of trust.

One or both of you wants to improve the other.

This means you're viewing your beloved, or your love relationship, as a project. That is not how an adult love relationship works.

You need to stop allowing him to lie to you for the most trivial reasons and destroying the belief you have in him.

It is important to give them space but not when they are misusing it.

You are as valuable as the pearl found in the oysters.

Never give the power to anyone to tell you that you are weak because you are born with that courage.

Love is fragile but you are strong, don't ever forget that.

12

The Third Angle

When people tell me that they broke up because of a multitude of reasons, sometimes one of them it's the third person.

He cheated on you with another woman so you blame the third person for snatching him from you. If love was a commodity, anyone could have come and taken it. But it's not.

When someone is yours, you don't have to keep his loyalty in check. You don't have to be a detective and keep stalking his social network.

I got to know from a mutual friend that my partner had been getting really close to this new girl from his work place. I had no clue about it but I let that slide. Later he started hanging out with her secretly. I was very hurt. I thought of meeting the other woman but then I stopped myself.

Maybe she wasn't even aware of who I was. I realized that you cannot practically do anything when someone decides to cross all boundaries.

Blaming the third person for your break up is nothing less than absurd.

Your partner chose him over you. It is not like he has been influenced or put under some kind of a magic spell.

He willingly chose to spend time with her.

However much you can be adamant that the third person tried to snatch your partner but the reality will remain that he never loved you enough in the first place.

When people break up it's never any reason that I can agree with.

In my opinion there is only one reason people separate and that's the lack of will to love each other no matter what.

Because when it's the right kind of love, you won't have to find the will every day. Everything will fall into place.

13

Just Toxic Things

The relationship has run its course and he took you as a liability. When things get out of hand, you leave it.

You don't try to find an excuse for people hurting you. Many women as well as men go through this. They take abuse and call it love. Let me check you right there. Love isn't abuse. You don't hit people if you love them. You don't abuse people you care about.

When you are nice to them but all they do is hit you or demean you by throwing abuses at you, you should know it's something seriously wrong with your relationship.

If they love you, they will kill anything literally that comes close to even hurting you intentionally. They won't hurt you and call it love.

When you are behaving like what your partner wants, he is the sweetest guy on the planet but when you want to be who you are in real you see him changing.

When you don't meet the list of requirements he has of you, he becomes impatient and it leads to an array of arguments. When you don't dance to his tunes, he regrets even dating you.

He hits you and calls it love. He throws you across the room and wipes away your blood from your bruised head. When you want to break free he gets you the sweetest gifts and you decide to stay. You don't DESERVE THIS. I don't think I can stress this enough. You do not deserve a love that leaves your soul lifeless and your heart loveless. You are so much more.

Abuse doesn't only have to be physical. Do not believe when they say that they don't know how to handle love and they are still learning. You are not their experiment.

There are so many men and women who are suffering mental abuse and torture in the name of love. You all deserve love.

You all deserve love.
You are not alone.

Don't let your weakness blind you to keep the devil in your life. You are made for better things. Better places. Better people. Happiness is waiting for you. Just take a step. Make an effort.

It is time you unlock your cage.
Fly away. Fly high.
Do not look back.

What has broken you cannot fix you.
Not now, Not ever.

They do not love you.
They love the power they have over you.
 Your mind. Your body.
Take that power away from them.

Only one person can have that power and that is you. Slam the door on their faces.

Show them who you are. Claim your lost self-respect. It is never too late to begin.

Toxic relationships will only pull you down and at one point they will drive you to kill yourself.

I have been in that zone. It sucked the life out of me. I did not even know who I was and that proved one thing. It had made me lose me. That is when I decided to quit.

I don't care if your mother or father or any extended family member also has endured abuse and refer to it as normal. Don't believe that.

No one deserves to go through abuse. Not me, Not you and Not anyone.

No one is worth ending the soul in you.

14

Instincts Always

You don't believe this when I say but you should always trust your intuition. Your gut instincts about your partner are cent percent true.

If you feel he is having an affair and that's why he is neglecting you, yes in most of the cases he is.

If you feel he is not yet ready for a commitment, most of the times he is not.

Don't sugarcoat your intuitions. Don't tell yourself he doesn't mean what he says. Don't cover up by saying that he is still trying to figure out his life and once it is figured out he will change.

Trusting your intuition is safeguarding your heart against misuse and there is nothing wrong with that.

It is easy.

If you feel that you are attracting negative vibes by being with someone, you need to cut it off. It does not matter it is your significant partner or even any family member. If they are not adding any value to your life, making you feel good, constantly complaining just cut it off.

When something negative happens, we tend to blame our partners. We although are equally at fault for letting it still exist in our lives.

We often choose to see everyone with rose tinted glasses and perceive them just how we see them, not who they actually are. If you are having a strong feeling that something is nor right, then this is a sign. The universe cannot come and save you if you choose to ignore the blessings. Don't cross question it. Don't shun it. Don't feel like you are overthinking. Because you are not.

We all possess that sixth sense and that's there to guide us. To fulfil our souls. To lead us on the road of love. To be the friend we need when we don't even have ourselves. We always get hints when something is not happening the way we would have wanted. Yet we choose to ignore it. We decide not to see it knowingly.

Our heart knows it all too well before we do.

Yet we choose to let ourselves go through the pain, the betrayal, the lies, the loneliness. All because we are too afraid to trust our instincts. We feel if all that we know comes true then it will break us. It will tear us apart. It will lead to another failed relationship. Another loss. Another tear.

So what.

Is it okay to keep people in our lives even if they are bad for our mental health?

Is it okay to keep loving them although they treat us like we don't even exist?

Don't let love become your prison. It should be your doorway to the realms of freedom.

If we choose to embrace and trust what our minds think and hearts feel then, we shall see the light.

We shall have hope for a miracle.

We can love again.

We could grow again

Without them

Without the critique and hatred.

Just like we deserve to live, brave and happy.

15

Some Insecurity

It is natural for you to get jealous sometimes and feel insecure. All those books preaching that being insecure is wrong, I fairly do not agree with that.

Because where there is understanding, there will be no place for insecurity in the first place.

If you are in love with someone it's obvious that you will feel insecure when you see them giving the same attention they once gave to you.

You are human and you feel fear at the thought of them being with someone else. It is your partner's job to never ever let that fear get to your heart and never let that fear control your relationship. It should be their priority to make you feel safe.

Any relationship takes time to build. Trust takes time. If words don't meet actions, then why are you even with him in the first place.

You are always frank with him regarding your life and your friend circle, but if he is hiding things from you and not communicating in a transparent way then you need to re-evaluate everything you have with him.

Instead of taking the blame of being insecure you should tell him to stop making you feel that way.

It is obvious you would feel insecure if he chooses spending time with others over you every time. Do not buy the theory that he needs space and that is why he is behaving like that.

If he cannot handle your love in a matured way and uses your vulnerability against you, you are with the wrong partner.

Any relationship demands mutual faith. If you are feeling paranoid its him who will fix this and do what it takes to help you feel heard.

To remove all your doubts.
To never leave you hanging there by a thread of fear.
It isn't too hard to keep things going good.
Transparency is key.

16

Never Good Enough

You can buy new clothes. You can change your hairstyle. You can even join the dance classes. You can try what you may, but you will still be average for him.

You can even go to the extent of being exactly as he wants. You just cannot satisfy him. There is always one thing or the other.

Today it is your vibrant nature that he cannot tolerate anymore. Tomorrow it is going to be your friend circle. In the future it might even be your family.

Slowly you start feeding his ego by making changes in your personality. Why are you doing that? Is that making you happy?

You are not his improvement assignment.
You are not anyone's wellness project.

The only person you should be good enough for is yourself. And you already are that. You are capable of so much more that you just cannot see.

Love can find you when you are at your breaking point.

Love can find you when you are flying high with success. It doesn't discriminate and tell you to change your personality accordingly.

You do not need guidelines or instructions to make someone fall in love with you.

No goodness will ever be enough to keep a man hooked on to you.

No beauty will ever be enough to keep him addicted either. You know what would be the most attractive asset to keep your partner attracted in the long run?

Well, nothing. Love is not some kind of a competition. You don't have to be good enough for anyone to be in love with you. When someone genuinely wants you, you will be good enough even when you will try all the ways to make him believe why you are flawed.

In the eyes of the right person you are already your best version without even trying.

17

Enough Is Enough

When you are always saying yes, you are giving them the hint that you are submissive. Why should they respect you then?

You are not responsible for their actions. But you are responsible for how much space they are occupying in your life.

You think saying no is hard.
Yes, it is one of the hardest things you will ever do in your life.

It will cost you relationships.

You know what it will not cost.

It won't cost you your happiness.

It won't cost you your mental health.

It won't cost you your inner peace.

Saying no might sting now. And that is what happens to people with good hearts. When you have a heart that's forgiving and too caring about the needs of others you forget that you exist too. You are continuously placing others before you. You are always concerned about making others happy and that is a beautiful trait. But it's important to know who are the ones worth suffering for.

Not everyone can value a good heart as you.

A good soul as you.

A positive energy like you deserves to be handed over to someone who knows how to treasure you.

Not someone who still hasn't found your true value.

Old wounds take time to heal. But once they heal, you don't feel the pain anymore. This too shall pass.

If saying no to a bad relationship makes you say yes to a brighter relationship with yourself then do that.

Don't wait for him to end it with you. Sometimes it's important you take the plunge in the deep waters.

You might sink. You might float. But you will learn to swim.

You will learn what is love.

You are the right definition of love.

You are magic.

Once you break free only then you can soar high into the wide open sky.

Nothing tastes sweeter than the freedom you find

Outside the cages of broken promises

For nothing good will be ever flourish

In familiar strangers you once called your home

PART 2

Revival

1

Where Do I Go From Here?

Nowhere.

Everywhere.

The answer in within you. You have to make that choice. You either stay stagnant. You can keep thinking about why did nothing work out for you.

Or you have another choice.

You pick yourself up, look into the mirror. Tell yourself it is not over. Maybe that person's role in your story is over but life definitely isn't.

The first choice is easy. Easy things in life hardly teach you lessons.

Also don't regret.

Regret will not solve anything.
They left you. You were so nice to them, you meant every word you said and yet they left. You chose to give love.

It is the sign of pure intentions.

Not everyone can love with a love so deep and a loyalty that does not change sides.

It is the reflection of how contagious your energy is.

No one can make you feel bad over that. What has happened, it is going to remain in your past. That does not define your present. It cannot mark a territory over your future.

You fell in love for a reason and things did not work out. It is okay.

Even if life seems over and you have no reason to look forward to another day it is okay.

Feel proud that you are out of it now.

Give yourself the credit for choosing yourself before them.

It will be your toughest battle maybe but that's what life is. You fight. You win or you lose. But don't you ever give up because if you don't, then your sorrows are going to smile at you and nothing can break you apart anymore.

Things will change

It takes time for the flower to bloom

You will shed your skin

Every inch part by part

Be patient , be brave

Make mistakes, many mistakes

Before your soul decides its prepared to love

Selfless and Carefree

2

Why Me?

Just take it this way. It could have been anyone. But you are the special one. You are chosen to go through this by the universe.

When I dropped out of the two colleges one after the other, people used to mock me, talk behind my back. They made fun of the fact that I was a dropout. No one understood what were the struggles I went through. I was going through a bad break up. I was molested by someone I called my friend. I was losing the relationship I had with my parents. I had become so occupied by all this that I lost track of why I was living. I had lost my purpose. I did not know why I was stuck always with the wrong partner. I was frustrated that I could never express what I was feeling. Each time I wanted to open up to someone, something held me back. It was some kind of a fear. Some kind of an anxiety. I never deserved what I had been through. Yet I went through that. I remember crying over almost anything. I was losing grip slowly and then all at once.

When you have been through abuse and so much hurt, being brave doesn't come easy. I decided to cry for once and let it go. You cannot be brave until and unless that is the sole option you have. I had no alternatives. I failed miserably at killing myself. I was so consumed by feelings of hatred towards myself that I forgot to notice I am made of love.

Courage is something that you cannot learn. You already have it in your soul. The challenge is to bring it out when you need it the most. Reconnecting to your soul is the first form of love. I decided to give this a shot. We often look for that one ray of hope when we are struggling the most. That one helping hand that will pull you out of the mess.

You do not need anyone to save you.

You only need you.

You are enough.

The universe puts you through so much so that you realize who you are. You can achieve so much. Don't let the failures define you. Never take any loss to your heart.

Anything can be overcome. Break ups. Divorces. Bad grades. Unemployment. Literally anything. Keep the hope alive.

The kindness you have is so raw and real that it is tempting.

Do not let anything come even close to disrupting that or stopping you from growing.

Not everyone has the ability to empathise

Not everyone can assure the soul of renewal

Not everyone can hold themselves together when they are falling

apart

Not everyone can have the strength when they face their

demons

You are chosen because you are.

It is you because you deserve to tell your story to the ones who need to hear the most.

You deserve to make a change by empowering others to unlock their real selves. Feel proud you could overcome those setbacks.

You could finally conquer over your fears.Don't ask why it is you.

Be thankful it is you as you are now finally yourself.

3

Missing Him

Many times you miss your partner once you don't have him anymore. You accuse yourself of missing him and that is unhealthy for you. Accusing yourself for loving him is only going to make you feel worse.

You loved him with all you had. You were not wrong in the way you loved. That is your beauty. That is your vibe.

Missing someone is okay. It's okay to feel empty without that person because that's how you feel when you lose someone who took so much space in your life. It's okay to feel shattered for a while. Give yourself that space. It's okay to feel hurt.

What's not okay is to put the blame on yourself for still missing him.

It's not your fault that he turned out to be everything that he never said he would be.

It's not your fault that he let you down and walked over your crushed soul.

It is important to know that it's fine to miss people. There is nothing wrong with it. Because you don't actually miss them but you miss what you had.

I won't remember your face one day

I won't remember the way you embraced me

I won't remember your marks on my body

You will remember me

When you're tired and all alone

When you'll reach out for me

But you won't find me

You'll miss me when you'll know I'm gone

But you won't find me

4

Pain

When you go through pain after a heartbreak , don't ever let that harden you . Your heart is gold and irrespective of his actions you kept loving him till you could not take it anymore.

Breaking up is painful, so don't try to fight your tears.
 Don't try to forget.
Don't run away.

They might have broken their promises but you cannot break your soul thinking of that.

Pain is inevitable. If you will love, you will feel hurt.

The difference is that the right person will not let you feel it all alone. Loving won't be a burden. It will be a necessity because he has your heart in his hands and nothing will make him toss that.

If you want to hide in a corner and not talk to anyone for some time, do that.

Take your time to feel this pain wholeheartedly.
Feeling and accepting it is what keeps us going.
Don't try finding other alternatives to not feel it.
Don't drink away your problems.
Don't smoke away the stress.

What you need is not whiskey, but a remedy for the soul.

Today you'll feel the pain.

Then you will accept it. And tomorrow you will be at peace.

They hurt you and filled your heart with pain.

It is time you release that hurt. Let go of the pain as it no longer deserves to be there.

Give yourself the space to recover from the trauma.

You shall heal with time. Don't let the pain of yesterday harden you. Let it all be gone.

You will fix yourself. You don't need medication to cope with it. Once you let yourself connect with the reason you are hurt, you will realize how powerful you are. Wounded birds learn to fly too. You just need to figure out how .

5

Drunk Love

If your ex is drunk and he calls you saying that he misses you, run for your life . There is no second meaning for it.

If he doesn't think about you when he is sober, you are better off being single rather than being on his drunk dial list.

You don't have to over analyze and think that why he called you and maybe he actually loves you. Because he doesn't. He is just finding a way to get into your pants as he is consumed by lust. Since he knows your weaknesses, he will always use them against you. So it's pointless falling for his tears or buying his sob stories as it's all going to end in vain.

Some people just treat love as a game. I have met such men and all I can say is you will never know their true colors before it is too late. When my ex used to get drunk, he would call me and tell me how much he missed me. I used to get emotionally unstable and would call him up next day and he would not even talk to me now. This happened few times and then I finally cut him off. You just . I don't care what anyone says but if they loved me so much then they would have still been with me .

If you are confused whether they still miss you, yes they do. They miss the way you were always available.

You cannot keep yourself whole because each time you take his drunk calls, you are lowering your self esteem inch by inch. Don't do that to yourself. He was never meant to be with you and he never bothered about you.

Make a vow to yourself, to only entertain love when its sober.

6

Mixed Feelings

Many a times you might feel overwhelmed by emotions .
Sometimes you might hate him for breaking your heart and
the other times you might miss him so much that your entire
body hurts.

You don't have to stay trapped there. You are allowed to
have mixed feelings. It's okay. We all have been there.

You might look at your old photographs and have
emotional outbursts. You might feel anger. You might feel
pain.

You might not want to even stay in the same house you
once shared with him.

There will be days you will want to see if he is doing fine. There will be nights you will stay up crying all because you long for him.

But then you will understand that you are only longing for something that's unattainable.

Someone that's not even bothered about you.

Something that's not even there. Something that was never real.

Because in love, you don't feel abandoned.

Allow yourself to feel these emotions till it's finally the arrival of something new and that's you.

7

Taking Him Back

He left you without even thinking once about you. He did not even care once to not break you apart. You kept promising yourself that he is the man you will marry or see you a future with. And it just took him a moment to end it all. Now that he doesn't have your attention he is feeling like a fish out of water and he wants you back.

He will try calling you and even go to the extent of begging you and try every way to win you back.

You will feel weak at times .You will want to get back with him .

Always remember never go back to the place that destroyed you because nothing good will ever grow there .

You will only feel the pain more intensely and even if you want to start a fresh chapter and leave everything behind, it's better you change the book.

Never let the same thorn prick you again.

The wound only gets worse with time.

The right man wouldn't lose you in the first place and if he does even have a chance of losing you he will make up for it while having you in his life. He won't let such a situation arise where youl'l be thinking to call you quits.

Absence makes the heart grow fonder but it can also make you realize your value in someone's life.

If he only misses you when you're absent in his life and misuses you when you're present it's not worthy of being called love.

8

Wish Him Pain

When I broke up with the man I was with , I was left with a crushed spirit

There were so many answers I needed. I needed closure. I needed to know why I was so badly hurt. I was ashamed of what I had allowed to happen to me. In my mind, he was the one that did me wrong and I wanted him to suffer so bad.

Not once did I think he would change me into someone so harsh. I had started hating the word love and everything even remotely associated to it.

I used to feel broken and even stupid for falling for him. I started hating myself for trusting him. And then something happened. He stopped crossing my mind. I also realized I need to stop feeling that I am a victim. That's not who I am. I chose to be with him. I made a mistake. I learnt. That's it.

I had to go through the pain so that I could know what betrayal feels like.

I had thought on multiple occasions of wishing that he goes through the same pain that I went through.

But something stopped me from within and that was the goodness within me So I made the choice to quit wishing him pain, rather I would wish him the healing he needs and let it all go.

Wishing him pain and bad vibes would only destroy my inner essence. It's easier to wish something bad but it's tougher to wish that person the healing he needs.

Not everyone can be kind and giving even after being hurt.

Try to wish him only healing as that's what will help you cope with the reality.

You don't have to be in touch with them. You can be friends with you ex but from far. And only if he was never toxic with you.

Before you decide whether to be friends with them, analyze the kind of relationship you had with them and also how it can impact your future.

Some people just deserve to stay away. It is as clear as that.

Keeping all these feelings bottled up inside you is going to be harmful so let it out one by one, slowly and kindly.

First take care of your heart and detox your soul by letting him go, all of him.

Negativity has a habit of creeping up on you when you are at your worst. Don't let your life be at its beck and call.

9
Love
Unconditionally

If you want a love that's unconditional it's not wrong. Because that's what love is.

It's not a feeling with conditions. There will be no restrictions when you are in love with the right man.

You see his changed behavior and you feel you can change him. You will try every way to get the old days back.

But there is no mechanism to receive love.

It does not have a set of rules. There is only one rule and that is simple. You should always love with all your heart and put everything you can to keep it real but only if it's from both the sides.

One sided love sounds beautiful but nothing stings more than the heartbreak you endure in this.

You allow him to be with you with conditions and that's the worst you can bring upon yourself.

Love doesn't have to be earned by not being yourself.

Love doesn't have to be proven by living a lie.

When someone truly loves you, they love you for who you are, not for what you do.

Love is consistent. That doesn't mean that in love they are never triggered, but they take responsibility for their triggers and apologize when they've acted out.

Underneath the trigger, you can feel the river of love that never stops flowing.

Handsome is what handsome does .

Love is what love does.

You don't have to meet someone's conditions so that they love you.

You don't have to be so doubtful if you're worth it or not.

10
Will I Ever Forget him?

No you won't.

I won't lie to you.

If you have really cared for them and loved them, you won't.

Every time you cross the place where you hanged out and drank coffee you will think about him.

Every place you have gone together will remind of you him.

Every memory you have of him will haunt your days and nights.

Every time you see his shirt in the drawers of your cupboard that you had gifted him, you will miss him. You will reopen the gifts he gave you and feel a lump in your throat every time.

You will feel yourself drifting away from his thoughts slowly.

You will eventually start coming out of your shell and meeting up with yourself once again.

Now when anyone mentions his name, you will not cry anymore.

But you will smile and thank him for giving you back to you.

It will take time but you will forget him fragment by fragment. And that's nothing to be ashamed of.

Not everyone loves with a love so deep and with a soul that's so graceful.

Gradually he will just be a face you used to know.

You will no longer feel the hurt even. You will grow past your mistakes. You will finally know why it ended . You will know all the answers to the questions he never had an answer for.

When the right person arrives he will make sure you get an ocean of love and happiness and you will only feel how blessed you are that you were bold when it was needed.

11

Face The World

A lot of times we are scared to face anyone once we break up or fall apart.

A lot of suggestions that I got during the hard times in my life were to be brave, face everyone right then no matter how broken up I was from inside.

I never advise this to anyone.

I feel it's important to face yourself first.
Only if you can feel everything deeply, you can face yourself. The world can wait. So first get rid of your fears.

What will your friends think of your break up?

What will your family think of your break up?

How will you face everyone now that you're single?

All these questions are not important.

The only significant thing that matters is how you see yourself.
You can face the world when you feel you are prepared. No rush. No fear.

If you need the time to come out of your hiding place, do that. Take that time.

Butterflies do it all the time and once they are out of their cocoons their beauty is unparalleled.

12

The Judgement Hour

It is during these trying times that we come to know the true colors of our friends and even family to a huge extent.
If your friends start changing sides and start analyzing your character just because you are going through a break up, they are better off as strangers.

Because friends don't do that. True friends stand by you like your rock and when you fall in deep water they will be your anchor.
If you have a family member that tells you to change yourself to suit to his needs or maybe be a prettier version of yourself, then you need to cut off such ties for good.

You are your own judge.

You broke up because you loved yourself more than this relationship. You broke up because you wanted to move on to better things. You broke up because your mind wanted to be liberated . You needed this. Don't let your friends decide everything for you. They might know what's good for you but you will know what's right for you.

Don't ever give that choice to others to judge you or tell you how you could have saved your relationship.

It's always easier said than done. It is easier to comment on others rather than walking in their shoes.

Design your life like how you want, not how others want you to live it. You just live once. Own it. Rule it.

13

I Can Never Love Again

The most beautiful thing about break ups is that they teach your life.

They teach you loneliness is not crazy.

They teach you self-respect is important.

They teach you being kind to yourself no matter what.

They teach you to appreciate your demons without any compromise.

This process takes time because you're on the road to write a brand new chapter and that's called self-love.

Love is very simple. It's us humans who complicate it.

Once you break up you decide you won't love again and that's wrong.

Because you can never decide when it's time for you to fall in love. It does not happen like that. When love happens you will be totally unaware. You won't hide yourself behind the veils of fear and insecurity anymore.

It's like the bright sunlight that touches your skin.

It's the sound of the river that pours tranquility into your soul.
 It is not you who has the power to choose that.

Love doesn't happen in a planned way.

And when it happens you won't stop yourself because it will be worth only one thing and that's your happiness.

You just need to give love a chance.

Give life a chance.

It is okay to feel scared.
Maybe for a day or maybe for a while.

Never stop believing in miracles. Anything can happen.
You cannot slam the door on the face of life.

Even if you are single now, you cannot let one person ruin what the future has got for you. You cannot let one individual dominate over your life.

It is your time to shine now. This is your chance at life.

14

Good People

Many of us feel that once we endure a heartbreak, we can never feel the same feelings again. What you are doing here is mixing up your feelings of love with feelings of anxiety.

What if he is not the one?

What if he abandons me too?

What if he betrays you too?

What if he just is like all the other people I have been with?

To protect yourself from getting hurt you build up walls around your soul.

You stop letting anyone near you. You think the world is full of people like the ones that have hurt you and stabbed you in the back.

We were in love with people who were not good for us.

That does not change the way we love.
That does not change the heart we possess.
That does not alter anything in fact.

When you will come across the soul that resonates at the same vibrancy you shall feel everything too deeply.

You need to have faith that not everyone is here to break your soul and crush your spirit.

There will be better faces and better places in the future that will take you for you, pick you up and walk with you. That's what you need in life.

Good energy. Higher vibes. Something meaningful.

Something that addresses all the wrongs done to you and changes them into rights.

Some kind of hope that keeps telling you that you can't give up yet.

There is always something good that happens when something bad ends.

Where there is drought, the rains will arrive sooner or later. Where there are sorrows, smiles shall arrive now or later. Don't doubt the process in which the universe works.

You are here for a reason.
It is not by chance that you have gone through the heartbreak or the pain.

It is not by chance that you have accepted that phase.

It is not by chance your soul is healing now.

Behind everything is some force that is trying to tell you
that no matter what happens in the future, it has got you.

You are never alone. You got yourself.

You know how to love better now. You know how to love
yourself, the scars and your past.

This is the sign you have been looking for.

15

Before Him

Before you were his, you were the universe's child.

You represent the moon, the stars and galaxies of unexpressed desires.

You were never meant to be tamed.

You are born free. You are wild.

Yes, you let him alter your vibe. But you still got that light.

No matter how many hands have touched you, you are pure.

You can be who you want.

There is no fear anymore.

Expand your horizon.

Don't measure how much you can fly. Just fly. Flawlessly flawed and imperfectly perfect.

If you have yourself, you have everything. You don't need any one to show you the way. You make your own. Rules and ways.

You always have so much goodness within you. It radiates. It surrounds everyone who comes close. Your bones no longer ache thinking of anyone that tried to destroy that.

You must fly finally to a place called home

Where everything shines

And nothing reminds her of the cage

Her wings might be in despair

But with a resolution so strong

Nothing seems to stop her now

With new wings she will fly to another reality

No more fears

Only love and strength

Where you are valued and are safe

Don't ever let go without feeling the pain

Don't ever move on without knowing your worth

Don't ever let it break your strength

And that's how you'll be unhurt

The skies still seem grey

You want to give up

You can again climb those mountains

You can again swim the oceans

Cause you are fierce

Cause you are still vulnerable

Cause you are exactly where you should be

In the arms of love and that's you

26158297R00074

Printed in Poland
by Amazon Fulfillment
Poland Sp. z o.o., Wrocław